40 Days

A Forty Day Journey
On Your New Commitment
With Christ

By Pastor Todd Smith

ISBN: 978-0-87148-464-2

Printed by Derek Press, Cleveland Tennessee

DEDICATION

This book is lovingly dedicated to the best friend I have ever had, my Dad. Words cannot express the love and admiration I have for him. When I was a young boy I would watch and wait for him to come home from work. Why? I wanted to play. I will never forget the times of throwing the ball, wrestling on the floor, laughing together and more recently, days of fishing. Obviously, I am no longer a young child, but my desire to see him and play with him is as strong today as ever.

Through the years, my dad taught me how to be a winner. He taught me to never give up and to always be a man of honesty and integrity.

Dad, thanks for giving me your best, your time and your heart. I am where I am today because of you. I love you!

Your son,
Todd

CONTENTS

READ THIS FIRST!

Welcome to the greatest 40 days you have ever lived!

Whether you have recently made the decision to follow Christ, or whether you have been a believer for many years, this study book is for you. At times, we all have questions, concerns or even apprehensions regarding our Christian walk. This study was designed to establish basic truths, answer questions and set you on a steady course in your adventure with God. The Christian life is a life of constant growing, maturing and developing. Believe me, *no one* has "arrived."

Please know, there is nothing you could do to cause Jesus to love you any more than He does right now! We do not follow Him, study His Word, pray or even serve Him in order to gain His acceptance. God told Jeremiah He had set him aside for a special purpose *long before* he was even born. The same holds true for you! So, relax and realize now that you are not striving for His acceptance or attention. Rest assured, you've got His attention.

Set your heart to simply enjoy building and enhancing your relationship with Him because He *wants* you to, not because you *have* to. Please realize that your relationship with Jesus is the most important one you have. Take it seriously and commit to be faithful in your pursuit of Him. Just as any person would expect his/her spouse to be completely faithful in a covenant relationship, God expects faithfulness as well.

That brings me to the title of this book, *"40 Days."* You may wonder why this name was chosen. The fact is, the number forty is extremely significant throughout the Bible. Forty is the number used by God to represent a *period of testing during which God's grace is experienced and revival and a new beginning are the end result!* The word "forty" appears 146 times in the Scriptures and often refers to spiritually significant times when God was *preparing someone for His purpose.* Let me give you some examples:

- In Noah's day, the rain fell for forty days and nights (Gen. 7:12)
- Moses was with God on Mt. Sinai forty days and nights (Ex. 24:18)
- The entire city of Nineveh was transformed when God gave the people forty days to turn to Him (Jonah 3:4)
- Jesus fasted forty days and nights before He began His earthly ministry (Matt. 4:2)
- Jesus was tempted forty days in the wilderness upon the announcement of His divine purpose (Luke 4:2)
- Jesus remained on the earth after his resurrection for forty days in order to instruct His disciples before He returned to the Father (Acts 1:3)

Noah obeyed God and built the ark in spite of the ridicule and questioning of others and as a result, **confidence** in God's promises was developed in him. Moses spent 40 days in God's presence and was presented with **divine direction** from Him. The city of Nineveh experienced the **grace** of God as He allowed them forty days to find their way to Him.

Consider Jesus Himself. In Luke 3:22, God the Father announced to the whole world, *"You are My beloved Son; in You I am well pleased."* Immediately Jesus entered the wilderness, spent forty days in the presence of the Spirit of God and, *"...returned in the **power of the Holy Spirit** to Galilee,"* ready to step into what God had for His life!

How does this relate to you? God wants to prepare you for a specific purpose as He did these individuals. During their times of testing, they developed certain characteristics, strengths and even habits that empowered them to face what God had for them to do. Foundations were laid in their lives. Truths were established. Convictions were grounded.

Just as a skyscraper is solidly built and cannot be moved, your faith will be set on a stronger foundation after you complete this book study, *"40 Days."* As you travel through the next forty days and beyond, you too will experience what the above individuals experienced *and more!* Confidence in God's Word and who He is will come to you. He will provide divine direction and you will experience His grace in times of need. And finally, you will be empowered as Jesus was to do exactly what it is He has purposed you to do!

How exciting! Do you realize what is in store for you? The next forty days promise to be life changing if you will commit to "stick with it" and allow God to transform your life as you walk through each page. Ask the Holy Spirit to teach you and allow Him to touch every area of your life. Without a doubt, transformation will come....

WEEK ONE
(Days 1-7)

Below are some activities that will enhance your new walk with Christ. When you complete the below assignments, check the appropriate box.

☐ Memory Verse – Philippians 4:13

> *"I can do all things through Christ who strengthens me."* *(NKJV)*

☐ Church Attendance

Church attended _____

☐ Find a Prayer Partner

☐ Prayer Requests

_____

_____

_____

_____

MY NEW HEART

Wouldn't it be wonderful to be able to trade in your old heart for a new one? Just think about the possibilities. When your heartbeat becomes irregular, you simply request a new one and then off you go. Wow! Maybe our technology will make it happen in the near future. However, right now it is impossible. On the other hand, God is in the business of making old hearts new. In fact, when you became born again, God gave you a new heart and a new beginning on life.

"Therefore if any person is [ingrafted] in Christ, " the Messiah" he is a new creation (a new creature altogether); the old [previous moral and spiritual condition] has passed away. Behold, the **FRESH** *and* **NEW** *has come!"* 2 Corinthians 5:17 (Amplified)

Now that you are a Christian you can expect your life to change.

1. Look carefully at Colossians 2:6-7. How did you begin your new life in Jesus?

_____

2. Read Ephesians 2:1-5.

a. What was your spiritual condition before you were saved? (vv.1,5)

_____

b. Now what is your condition? (vv. 1,5)

_____

3. What has been the biggest change you have seen in your life since you came to know Christ?

_____

_____

_____

"God loves you just the way you are, but He refuses to leave you that way."
Max Lucado

4. What happened to your previous lifestyle? 2 Corinthians 5:17, Romans 6:6

_____

_____

5. How should one walk after he finds Christ? Romans 6:4

_____

_____

6. Read Philippians 3:13,14.

a. What should be our attitude toward the things in the past?

_____

_____

b. If that is true, then what should you be doing now?

_____

_____

_____

7. What are you now? John 1:12

_____

REFLECTION:
Spend the next few minutes in prayer and thank God for your life in Jesus.

THE POWER AND PURPOSE
OF WATER BAPTISM

Each follower of Christ must make a commitment to follow Him fully. One key step of being a Christ-follower is to be water baptized. There is nothing more beautiful than seeing a new believer get water baptized. In this study you will understand its purpose and meaning.

1. What one event launched Jesus into His earthly ministry? Luke 3:21-23

   _____

   _____

2. According to Jesus' example, what should follow shortly after you give your heart to Jesus? Acts 8:36-38

   _____

3. Read Matthew 28:19,20. You have a three-fold assignment given to you by Christ. List below.

a. (v. 19) _____

b. (v. 19) _____

c. (v. 20) _____

4. According to Mark 16:16, what should a person do before he/she is baptized?

   _____

   _____

"Baptism points back to the work of God,
and forward to the life of faith."
J. Alice Moryer

5. Read Acts 10:44-48. What question did Peter ask after Cornelius gave his heart to Jesus?

_____

_____

6. While Paul and Silas were in prison (Acts 16:25-34) they led the jailer to the Lord. What happened in verse 33?

_____

TRUTH
When you are water baptized you walk into the water. Next, you are immersed in the water, and then you come out of the water. Water baptism is a beautiful picture of the **death, burial** and **resurrection** of Jesus.

7. Why do you think it is important to be baptized with water?

_____

_____

_____

8. Read Romans 6:1-4.

a. What happened to the "old you" when you got saved and baptized?

_____

b. Now how should you walk?

_____

- Baptism is the first thing Jesus asked of His followers.

- If you have not been baptized, do so as soon as you can. This will enhance and help you in your walk with Jesus. Plus, it will be a witness to all your friends that you are now a Christ follower.

GOD 101

The Lord desires to reveal Himself to us each day. His goodness, grace and beauty are beyond our finite comprehension. Think about it. The God of the universe, the Creator of all the universe, desires to know me and have a relationship with me...wow! What a concept! What a privilege! This chapter attempts to get you acquainted with the God that loves you and saved you. Be prepared to be wowed and dazzled by who He is!

1. What do these scriptures teach about God?

Psalm 90:2 _____

_____

Isaiah 40:28 _____

_____

1 John 3:20 _____

_____

2. In Psalm 46:1 God is described as:

   a. My _____   b. My _____

   c. My _____

3. Match the statements with the correct verse.

   ___ Hebrews 13:5   a. I am the resurrection
   ___ John 8:12   b. I am the first and the last
   ___ John 11:25   c. I will never leave you
   ___ Revelation 1:11   d. There is nothing too hard for God
   ___ Jeremiah 32:17   e. I am the light of the world

4. According to 1 John 4:8, "God is _____."

5. What does Jeremiah 31:3 mean to you?

_____

_____

_____

6. Examine John 3:16. According to this verse, why did God send Jesus to the earth?

_____

_____

_____

_____

7. Read Acts 17:24. What does this verse say about God?

_____

_____

8. What is God's attitude toward us? 2 Peter 3:9

_____

_____

9. Examine Deuteronomy 7:9. What does this reveal about God's nature and character?

_____

_____

_____

10. In 1 Peter 1:15,16 God gives us a command. What is that command and why should we obey it?

_____

_____

_____

DEALING WITH YOUR PAST

Have you ever been haunted by the mistakes of the past? Everybody has. Many people suffer from depression, anxiety and stress over the sins in the past. In fact, some people are even suicidal. The good news is that Jesus has the power, ability and authority to break the chains of regret off your life. There is no sin that He cannot and will not forgive. This chapter will help you to receive His forgiveness.

1. Look up the word "forgive" in a dictionary.

_____

_____

_____

2. Put Psalm 86:5 in your own words.

_____

_____

_____

3. When you came to Jesus He forgave your sins. According to Micah 7:19, what does God say He did with them?

_____

_____

_____

4. Also, Psalm 103:10-12 gives us insight on how God deals with our sins. What does this verse tell us about our past?

_____

_____

_____

_____

_____

5. Read Romans 5:6-11 carefully.

a. According to these verses, when did Christ die for us?

   i. (v. 6) _____

  ii. (v. 8) _____

 iii. (v. 10) _____

b. Read verse 9 again. Now define "justify" from a dictionary.

_____

_____

_____

c. How are you viewed by God according to the above verses and definition?

_____

_____

_____

6. Read Isaiah 1:18. Describe what God does to us and our sins when we get saved?

_____

_____

_____

> *"If God forgives us, we must forgive ourselves.*
> *Otherwise it is almost like setting up ourselves as a*
> *higher tribunal than Him."*
> C.S. Lewis

7. What did Paul do in order to overcome his past? Philippians 3:13

_____

_____

_____

_____

8. How can you apply the above verse to your life?

_____

_____

_____

9. Read 2 Corinthians 5:17.

a. What do you think Paul meant by "old things?"

_____

_____

b. What should we be doing now?

_____

_____

_____

10. Think carefully about 1 John 1:9. How does this verse relate to your life?

_____

_____

_____

- Thank God right now for His grace and mercy.

- Praise Him because all of your past failures and sins are forgiven!

HOW DO I KNOW IF I AM SAVED?

You can know you are saved! That's right. Many people doubt their salvation. Some believers constantly wonder if they would make it to heaven if they died. As a result, they live in a state of fear and confusion. The Bible says in 1 Corinthians 14:33, "God is not the author of confusion." God doesn't want you to doubt your salvation experience. Perhaps some of you are struggling with this issue right now. After this study you will no longer wonder if you are born again. Remember He loves you and you are His child.

1. What must one do in order to be saved? John 3:3

   _____

   _____

2. What does Romans 10:9,10 show us about how to be saved?

   _____

   _____

   _____

3. Read Romans 10:13. In your own words explain this verse.

   _____

   _____

   _____

   _____

4. What does John 6:47 promise?

   _____

   _____

Note: Believing in Jesus involves more than just understanding in your mind who Jesus is. It involves not only your intellect, but your whole being. One must believe to the point of surrendering their life to Him.

5. Write down the date and age you were when you got saved. It is okay if you can't remember the exact date. The date is not

what is important, but rather the experience. Then, write where you were when you accepted Jesus and the person responsible for helping you find Christ.

_____

_____

_____

_____

6. In your understanding of salvation, what does it mean to "believe in Jesus?"

_____

_____

_____

_____

7. How do the following verses help us to realize that we know Christ as our Savior?

1 John 4:13 _____

_____

Romans 8:16-17 _____

_____

8. What does 1 John 5:12 mean?

_____

_____

9. What helps us to know we have eternal life? 1 John 5:13

_____

10. According to 2 Corinthians 5:17, what is the best way to determine if you or someone else is saved?

_____

_____

_____

_____

If you are doubting your salvation, then pray this prayer:

Dear Jesus, I know you love me. You shed Your blood and gave Your life for me. On the third day You arose from the grave. I need You in my life, but I am a sinner. Please forgive and cleanse me. I turn from my wicked lifestyle and I choose to follow You. Please come into my life. Save me now! I give You my entire life. I love You, Jesus, and thank you for saving me. In Jesus' name, Amen.

GOD'S VIEW OF YOU

According to the Bible, from the beginning of time God has had you on His mind. In fact, He is "crazy about you!" You are the apple of His eye. In Zephaniah 3:17 the Bible says, "He rejoices over you with singing." He is not your enemy. He is your friend. The scriptures below take a close look at the Father's heart. Enjoy.

1. In Psalm 139:13-16 David describes God's role in your creation.

a. (v. 13) What did God do? _____

_____

b. (v. 14) How are we made? _____

_____

c. (v. 15) How were you "put together?" _____

_____

2. Read Psalm 139:17,18. Put these two verses in your own words.

(v.17) _____

_____

(v. 18) _____

_____

3. Read John 3:16. What did God's love for you and the world cause Him to do?

_____

_____

_____

4. According to Jeremiah 29:11, God is thinking about you.

a. What is God *not* thinking about doing to you?

_____

b. What is God thinking about you?

_____

_____

5. Look closely at Romans 8:38-39. What can separate you from the love of Christ? _____

6. Zephaniah 3:17 lists five proactive and positive movements of God on your behalf. List them below.

"The Lord your God is with you, He is mighty to save. He will take great delight in you, He will quiet you with His love, He will rejoice over you with singing." (Zeph. 3:17 NIV)

a. _____

b. _____

c. _____

d. _____

e. _____

7. How does Romans 5:8 prove God's love to you?

_____

_____

8. According to Jeremiah 31:3, is God's love for you based upon your behavior? _____ yes _____ no. Describe in your own words what this verse means to you. _____

_____

_____

MY FRIEND, THE HOLY SPIRIT

Have you ever been abandoned, betrayed or neglected? No doubt at one time in your life you have felt the sting of isolation and loneliness. The Bible says God would never walk out on us or leave us alone (Hebrews 13:5). You may ask, "how is that possible?" This chapter reveals God's care and concern for us. God loves us so much that He has given us the person of the Holy Spirit to live inside of us.

1. Why was it necessary for Jesus to have to go back to heaven? John 16:7

    _____

    _____

2. Jesus promised his followers that the Father would give them a special gift. Describe that gift. John 14:16,26

    _____

    _____

    _____

3. Read 1 Corinthians 3:16 and 6:19.

    a. What is your body? _____

    _____

    b. Who lives inside you? _____

    _____

    c. To whom do you now belong? _____

4. According to John 16:8, what is the Holy Spirit's job upon the earth?

    a. _____   b. _____

        c. _____

5. Describe how the Holy Spirit helped you to realize your need for Jesus? Give examples.

_____

_____

_____

_____

6. Describe in detail how John 16:13-16 applies to your life.

_____

_____

_____

_____

7. According to Romans 8:9-11, how do you know that you are saved?

_____

8. Because the Holy Spirit lives inside you, what are some of the results? 2 Timothy 1:7

_____

_____

_____

9. The Holy Spirit is called by different names. List as many as you can below.

_____

_____

_____

WEEK TWO
(Days 8-14)

CONGRATULATIONS! You just completed your first week in *40 Days*. Continue on your pilgrimage. Complete the assignment below and check the appropriate box.

☐ Memory Verse – Acts 1:8

"But you shall receive power when the Holy Spirit has come upon you; and you shall be witnesses to Me in Jerusalem, and in all Judea and Samaria, and to the end of the earth..." (NKJV)

☐ Church Attendance

Church attended _____

How many times church attended _____

☐ Date scheduled to be baptized _____

☐ Name of Prayer Partner _____

☐ Prayer Requests

_____
_____
_____
_____

☐ Answered Prayers

_____
_____
_____
_____

THE POWER OF PRAYER

The greatest privilege given to man is the ability to talk to Father God. Think about it, God wants to hear from you every day. Your relationship with God is growing stronger because of your communication with Him. Remember, the more you pray the more God moves on your behalf. Stay faithful and seek His face.

1. Read Jeremiah 33:3 carefully and answer the following:

a. What does God want us to do?

_____

b. What will be the end result? _____

_____

2. In Psalm 34:4 David prayed. What was the outcome?

a. _____ b. _____

3. Look closely at Hebrew 4:16.

a. What is God's desire for us? _____

_____

b. Why? _____

4. Who helps us when we pray? Romans 8:26-27

_____

5. Take a thorough look at Philippians 4:6-7.

a. What are you encouraged to do about your life and the situations you face? (v. 6)

_____, _____

_____

b. In your own words, what does verse 7 mean to you?

_____

_____

_____

6. What are we instructed to do when praying? Mark 11:23-24

_____

a. What is God's promise? _____

7. Why is it important to forgive others? Mark 11:25-26

_____

8. According to John 15:7, Jesus tells us that two things are necessary in order to receive answers to our prayers. What are they?

a. _____

b. _____

9. In whose name must we pray? John 16:24 _____

10. Examine 1 John 5:14-15.

a. How must we pray? (v. 14) _____

b. What will guarantee that God will hear your prayers? _____

_____

c. How should this help you when you pray? (vv. 14,15)

_____

_____

11. Read Ephesians 3:20. In your own words, what is God able to do when we pray in faith? _____

_____

- Give thanks to God for the wonderful privilege of prayer.

- You can touch God and bring your needs to Him.

- Think about it. Your prayers can move the hands that move the world!

- Go ahead and spend some special time talking with Jesus.

GOD'S WORD AND YOU

Have you ever been on a trip and gotten lost? Then you know the feeling of desperation that accompanies the experience. However, the proper use of a road map could have prevented the whole thing. The Bible is like a road map. In fact, it is your life's road map. If you will read it and walk in its ways you will be safe, secure and blessed.

"Your word is a lamp to my feet
and a light to my path."
Psalm 119:105 (NKJV)

1. How was the Word of God written? 2 Timothy 3:16

_____

2. Read 1 Peter 2:2 carefully and in your own words write what this means to you.

_____

_____

_____

3. Who will help you understand the Bible? 1 Corinthians 2:12-13

_____

4. Research these scriptures and list what the Bible reveals about its purpose as described.

Hebrews 4:12 _____

Psalm 12:6 _____

Psalm 119:105 _____

Ephesians 6:17 _____

5. List the four reasons why the Bible is profitable.
   (2 Timothy 3:16)

Profitable for _____ (teaches you *What's Right*)

Profitable for _____ (teaches you *What's Not Right*)

Profitable for _____ (teaches you *How to Get Right*)

Profitable for _____ (teaches you *How to Stay Right*)

> ***"The Bible is the best book in the world. It contains
> more...than all the libraries I have seen."***
> John Adams, second President of the United States

6. In your own words, why is it important to read the Bible
   everyday? 2 Timothy 3:17

   _____
   _____
   _____

7. James 1:22 gives us a strong warning. What is it?

   _____

8. What is a man like who reads the Word of God and fails to
   obey it? James 1:23-24

   _____

> ***"A Bible that is falling apart probably
> belongs to someone who isn't"***
> Christian Johnson

9. What does the Bible say will happen to the person who obeys
   the Word of God?

a. James 1:25 _____

b. Psalms 1:1-3 _____

c. Joshua 1:8 _____

10. As a Christian, it is impossible to please God without faith
    (Hebrews 11:6). According to Romans 10:17, how does one
    build his/her faith?

    _____

11. Colossians 3:16 says, *"Let the word of Christ dwell in you
    richly...."* The word "dwell" means to inhabit, to occupy, to
    reside in." List four ways you can cause the Word of God to
    live inside you.

a. _____

b. _____

c. _____

d. _____

Plan to begin each day with the Word of God.

-   Pray right now and ask God to speak to you from His Word.

-   Ask Him for the strength to obey His Word.

-   Thank Him for His words of life that is food for your spirit.

"I believe the Bible is the best gift God has ever given to man."
Abraham Lincoln, 16th President of the United States

THE BAPTISM WITH THE HOLY SPIRIT (PART 1)

As you study the baptism with the Holy Spirit over the next four days, your heart will hunger and thirst for everything God has for you. Prepare yourself for a great move of the Spirit in your life. Earlier YOU learned that when you gave your heart to Jesus, the Holy Spirit came to live inside of you. This chapter, as well as the three that follow, will reveal God's desire for you to walk in the "power of the Spirit."

1. In John 20:21-22 Jesus appears to His disciples after the resurrection.

a. What did Jesus do to His disciples? (v.22)

_____

b. What did He say to them? (v. 22)

_____

When Jesus *breathed on them,* the disciples received the *indwelling presence* of the Holy Spirit. Their bodies became the temple of God (1 Corinthians 3:16).

> **"When you gave your life to Jesus, the Holy Spirit came to live on the inside of you. He now indwells you."**

2. After this, Jesus instructed His disciples to go to what city? Luke 24:49

_____

3. Why were they commanded to go to that city? Luke 24:49

_____

Remember: The disciples had already received the *indwelling presence* of the Holy Spirit. Now Jesus is commanding them to go and wait until they are *"endued with power"* by the Holy Spirit.

4. Obviously, there is a difference between the *indwelling presence* of the Holy Spirit and being *endued with power.* What do you think is the difference?

_____

_____

_____

_____

5. After the disciples reached Jerusalem, Jesus once again appeared to them. Read Acts 1:4-5. What did He say would happen to them?

_____

6. The word *baptize* means to "immerse," to "saturate," to "cover over." With what did Jesus say He would *baptize* us? Acts 1:5

_____

7. What does this mean to you?

_____

_____

_____

_____

8. Look carefully at Acts 1:8.

a. What does Jesus say you will receive when the Holy Spirit comes upon you?

_____

b. When you are saved the Holy Spirit immediately comes to live *within* you. According to Acts 1:8, when you are *baptized with the Holy Spirit,* the Holy Spirit comes _____ you.

c. What did Jesus say you would become when you receive the baptism with the Holy Spirit?

_____

"When you experience the baptism of the Holy Spirit, you will receive a new boldness and courage to witness for Christ."

-   Begin to ask God to create a hunger in you for more of Him.

"You have not because you ask not...."
James 4:2

THE BAPTISM WITH THE HOLY SPIRIT
(PART 2)

Yesterday in your study you learned why God wants to fill you with His Spirit. Today, the heart of God will continue to unfold as you study the scriptures. Before you begin, ask God to open up your heart so you can learn more about the Holy Spirit.

1. Read Acts 2:1-4. The disciples received the baptism of the Holy Spirit. What does verse four tell you that happened?

a. _____

b. _____

2. In Acts 2:38-39 Peter told the crowd that they, too, could experience the power of God. According to the passage, what must they do?

a. (v. 38) _____

b. (v. 38) _____

3. What would the people receive if they obeyed the first part of verse 38? _____

4. According to verse 39, for whom is the *gift of the Spirit*?

a._____   b. _____

c. _____   d. _____

*"God commands us to be filled with the Spirit,
and if we are not filled, it's because we are living
beneath our privileges."*
Dwight L. Moody

45

5. Read Acts 4:31-33. What happened when the disciples prayed?

a. (v. 31) _____

b. (v. 31) _____

c. (v. 31) _____

6. What did the disciples do as a result of being *filled with the Holy Spirit*? Acts 4:33

_____

_____

**"Remember the baptism of the Holy Spirit takes place
after you are saved. It is for you!"**

7. Read John 7:37-39.

a. (v. 37) What does Jesus want us to do? _____

_____

b. (v. 38) What will be the result? _____

_____

c. (v. 39) According to this verse, whom does Jesus want us to receive? _____

8. Who do you think qualifies for the baptism of the Holy Spirit?

_____ Just the good people in church
_____ Only pastors and missionaries
_____ Anybody who is thirsty for more of Jesus

9. Write below why you think you need to experience the baptism of the Holy Spirit?

_____

_____

_____

THE BAPTISM WITH THE HOLY SPIRIT
(PART 3)

Before Jesus began his ministry, John the Baptist baptized him in the Jordan River. After Jesus' baptism, the Bible says that the Holy Spirit descended upon Him (Matthew 3:16). Don't miss this-- before Jesus began His public ministry the Holy Spirit came upon Him. Throughout the New Testament you will find that all of the great men and women of God who operated in power had the same experience as Jesus, that is the baptism of the Holy Spirit! This study will prepare your heart to receive the Holy Spirit's power in your life.

1. According to Matthew 3:11, what does Jesus desire to do in your life?

_____

2. Read Acts 8:14-17. The Samaritans had received Jesus as their Savior through the preaching of Philip. Why did Peter and John go to them?

a. (v. 15) _____

b. (v. 17) What did Peter and John do? _____

_____

c. (v. 17) What happened next? _____

_____

In Acts 9, Saul of Tarsus was saved and changed when he encountered Jesus on the Damascus road. God told Saul to go to Damascus and wait. In the meantime, God spoke to Ananias and told him to go and minister to Saul.

3. Read Acts 9:17. Ananias tells Saul why God sent him. What were those reasons?

a. _____

b. _____

4. Why do you think it is necessary to be baptized with the Holy Spirit?

_____

_____

_____

_____

Please note that Saul was already saved and then he received the fullness of the Holy Spirit!

   "It is God's will that all of us experience the baptism with the Holy Spirit. It is a must if we are to walk in victory!"

5. Read Acts 10:44-48. Cornelius was listening to Peter proclaim the good news of the gospel. Explain what happened next.

_____

_____

_____

_____

6. In verse 45 the Holy Spirit is described as a _____.

7. In verse 46, what did Cornelius do after he experienced the baptism with the Holy Spirit?

_____

8. In verse 47 Peter was speaking salvation to the Gentiles. What did they have to do in order to be baptized with the Holy Spirit?

_____

9. Look closely at Acts 19:1-6. What question did Paul ask the people at Ephesus?

_____

10. After Paul led them to Jesus, what did he do next? (v. 5,6)

a. (v. 5) _____

b. (v. 6) _____

11. What happened after they were baptized with the Holy Spirit?

(v. 6) _____

_____

"Jesus wants to fill you with His POWER!"

THE BAPTISM WITH THE HOLY SPIRIT
(PART 4)

Are you hungry and thirsty for more of Him? You may be asking how you can experience this precious baptism with the Holy Spirit. Today you will learn how to receive and experience God's power in your life. Be prepared to never be the same again.

1. Read John 7:37-39. A key ingredient is mentioned in verse 37. What do you think it is?

_____

2. What does Matthew 5:6 mean to you?

_____

_____

_____

Make no mistake about it. If you want to be filled with God's Spirit, you must *thirst and hunger* for Him.

3. Take a look at Luke 11:13.

a. What does the Father want to give you?

_____

b. What must you do? _____

4. What did the Samaritans do after Peter and John laid hands on them? Acts 8:14-17

_____

TRUTH
God desires to give you this precious gift. He is waiting on you!

Let's review. Here is how you receive the baptism with the Holy Spirit.

51

A. Hunger and thirst after Him with all your heart.

B. Yield your life to Jesus - all of it. Hold nothing back.

C. Pray and ask Jesus for the gift of the Holy Spirit.

D. Receive this precious gift by faith.

PRAY THIS PRAYER

Dear Jesus, please forgive me for my sins. I ask You to cleanse my heart. I am thirsty for You. I am hungry for holiness, righteousness and purity. I know only You can satisfy my hunger.

I know I need Your power in my life. I need the baptism with the Holy Spirit. So right now Jesus, I ask You to fill me to overflowing with your power. Come, come Holy Spirit and fill me in Jesus' name. By faith, I receive the baptism with the Holy Spirit. Thank you for filling me. Thank you, Lord, for the new wine I am receiving now. Thank You for baptizing me with the Holy Spirit.

NOW...Begin to let your praises flow. Praise God, the resurrection power of God has entered your life. Praise Him from your spirit.

Here are the changes you will notice.

A. You will receive a supernatural prayer language (Acts 2:4).

B. You will have a greater desire to live holy before the Lord.

C. You will receive power to be His witness (Acts 1:8).

D. You will be bolder and more courageous in your witnessing for Jesus (Acts 4:31).

E. You will have an increased hunger for the Word of God (Matthew 5:6).

I'VE GOT TO TELL SOMEBODY!

Do you find it difficult to keep a juicy secret? Doesn't it just burn on the inside until you tell someone? Jesus is the best-kept secret in the world. Jesus is calling you to tell others about Him. Don't forget that Jesus wants to do the same in others as He did in you.

1. What is the necessary ingredient in order to become an effective witness for Jesus? Acts 1:8

    _____

2. Read 2 Corinthians 5:17-20.

a. What did Jesus do for us? (v. 17,18)

    _____

b. What ministry do you now have? (v. 18)

    _____

c. What has Christ committed to you? (v. 19)

    _____

d. Now that we are saved, we are now what? (v. 20)

    _____

e. What does this mean to you?

    _____

    _____

    _____

3. Everybody has a story to tell. When witnessing to your friends or even strangers, you can tell them what your life was like before Jesus, how you came to know Jesus and what He has done in your life since you have been saved.

    In John 9 Jesus healed a blind man. Find the verse in the story that describes the three components above.

a. Life before Jesus, verse _____.

b. How he met Jesus, verse _____.

c. The change in his life after meeting Jesus, verse _____.

d. How did the blind man describe his encounter with Jesus? (v. 25)

_____

_____

4. Why do you think it is important to tell others about Jesus?

_____

_____

_____

5. According to 1 Peter 3:15, how should I live? Check the appropriate answer or answers.

a. _____ Ready to sing   c. _____ Ready to go to church
b. _____ Ready to teach   d. _____ Ready to witness

6. Read 2 Corinthians 4:3-4 carefully.

a. How can we *VEIL* the gospel?

_____

_____

b. What happens to those we never tell about Jesus? (v. 3)

_____

_____

c. Who is the *"god of this world?"* (v. 4)

_____

d. What is he trying to do? (v. 4)

_____

e. What does God want to happen to your friends? (vv. 4,6)

_____

_____

_____

7. What does Proverbs 11:30 say about the one who wins souls?

_____

8. According to Matthew 28:19-20, whose responsibility is it to witness?

_____

9. What did Jesus call His disciples in Acts 1:8?

_____

10. List those people in your life to whom God would have you witness.

_____

_____

_____

- Right now ask God to prepare their hearts to receive Jesus.

- Furthermore, ask Him to give you the power and boldness to share Christ with them.

- Remember, you hold the keys to eternal life – unlock the door of their heart so they can come to Jesus.

WEEK THREE
(Days 15-21)

You are doing wonderful! This week of study will be most interesting. You will learn the devil's plan for your life and how you can defeat him. Stay faithful this week and watch God do the miraculous in your life. Once again complete the assignment below and check the appropriate box.

☐ Memory Verses

> *"Therefore, submit to God. Resist the devil and he will flee from you."* James 4:7 (NKJV)

> *"Blessed are the pure in heart, for they shall see God."* Matthew 5:8 (NKJV)

☐ Church Attendance

Church attended _____

How many times church attended _____

☐ Met with Prayer Partner

☐ Prayer Requests

_____

_____

_____

_____

☐ Answered Prayers

_____

_____

_____

_____

LET'S MEET MR. DEVIL
(PART 1)

According to the teachings of the New Testament, the devil is subject to the name of Jesus. There is no need to fear him. However, do not underestimate him or his power. He is a formidable foe. If you apply the lessons learned in this study, you will understand your enemy better and be poised for victory.

"The devil and me, we don't agree;
I hate him and he hates me."
Salvation Army Hymn

1. Why was Satan kicked out of heaven? (Isaiah 14:12-14)
_____
_____

2. In Genesis 3:1-5, Satan deceived Eve. How did he do this?
_____
_____
_____

"The devil always leaves a stink behind him."
Author Unknown

3. Examine 2 Corinthians 11:3. How did Satan win over Eve?
_____
_____

4. Read 1 Peter 5:8,9.

a. (v. 8) What are we instructed to do? _____
_____

b. (v. 8) Peter describes the devil as what? _____
_____

c. (v. 8) What does he want to do with you? _____

_____

d. (v. 9) What action must we take to insure that doesn't happen?

_____

_____

5. Define James 4:7 in your own words.

_____

_____

_____

_____

"If you don't open the door to the devil, he goes away."

6. What do the following verses tell you about Satan?

a. John 10:10 _____

_____

How has the devil tried to destroy you or someone you know?

_____

_____

_____

b. 2 Corinthians 4:3-4 _____

_____

c. John 8:44 _____

_____

d. 2 Corinthians 11:14 _____

_____

_____

7. Examine Ephesians 6:10-18. What instruction does verse
    eleven give us and why?

    _____

    _____

Define *"wiles."*

    _____

    _____

-   Go ahead and praise God that Jesus is your Savior, your name
    is written in the Lamb's Book of Life and that you are sealed
    by the Holy Spirit.

LET'S MEET MR. DEVIL
(PART 2)

Before you were saved the devil didn't worry about you. Now that you are a Christ-follower he is very upset. The Bible calls the devil your "adversary" (1 Peter 5:8). He is out to get you. Nothing would please him more than to cause you to stumble. However, the good news is that Jesus defeated him on the cross and because of Christ's victory, you can overcome any attack from the enemy.

1. According to Luke 8:12, what does Satan want to do to the person who hears the good news about Jesus?

_____

_____

_____

2. In this scripture, who is hell prepared for? Matthew 25:41

_____

3. Because of the death, burial and resurrection, what did Jesus do to Satan? Colossians 2:15

_____

_____

_____

4. What does the future hold for the devil? Revelation 20:10

_____

_____

5. Read Luke 9:1,2. What did Jesus give to His disciples?

_____

_____

6. In Luke 10:17, the seventy disciples that Jesus sent out to preach the Good News came back to Him with a remarkable report. What was that report?

_____

_____

7. What was Jesus' comment back to them? Luke 10:18

_____

_____

8. In Luke 10:19, what did Jesus give to His disciples?

_____

_____

_____

9. Do you believe you have the same authority and power that the early disciples had? _____ yes _____ no. Explain your answer.

_____

_____

_____

_____

10. Read Mark 16:14-18. Jesus instructed His disciples to go and preach the gospel. He also said that certain signs would follow them. What are those signs?

_____

_____

_____

_____

_____

-   Because Jesus lives on the inside of you, now you have power over all the works of the enemy.

-   Exercise that authority and don't be afraid. You are the light of the world!

OVERCOMING SIN
(PART 1)

You are confronted every day with opportunities to compromise your walk with God. This study will reveal the devil's plan for your life when it comes to sin.

1. When Cain's offering was refused by God, Cain became angry and jealous of his brother Abel. Read Genesis 4:7.

a. What position did sin take in Cain's life?

_____

b. What was it doing there? In other words, what did it want? (v. 7)

_____

_____

c. How should you relate to sin? (v. 7) _____

_____

2. List three temptations you know are at your heart's door.

a. _____

b. _____

c. _____

3. Sin has a purpose. According to Romans 6:12, what specifically does sin want to do in your life?

_____

_____

4. What are you instructed to do with your body?

Romans 6:13,14 _____

_____

Romans 12:1 _____

_____

5. Why do you think it is important to present your body to God?

_____

_____

_____

6. How did the believers overcome Satan in Revelation 12:11?

a. _____

b. _____

7. How can you apply Revelation 12:11 to your life?

_____

_____

_____

8. How does James 4:7 help you in your battle with sin?

_____

_____

9. What does Romans 8:37 call you?

_____

10. According to Philippians 4:13, what promise do you have from the Father?

_____

_____

_____

OVERCOMING SIN
(PART 2)

The Bible explains sin's objective for your life. Sin wants to destroy you and your influence. Make a commitment not to let sin live and reign in your life.

1. James 1:14,15 shows us how sin begins in our lives and its ultimate objective.

a. What do you do to cause temptations to come your way?

(v. 14) _____

_____

b. Who do you think does the "enticing?" _____

c. What happens when you yield to temptation?

_____

_____

d. According to verse 15, is it true that sin wants to "grow" and be "more influential" in your life? _____ yes _____ no

e. What is sin's ultimate desire for you? (v. 15)

_____

_____

2. It is possible to live in victory over sin. What does 1 John 5:4,5 mean to you?

_____

_____

_____

3. In Psalm 119:11, what can you do in order not to sin?

_____

_____

4. What steps can you take in order to activate Psalm 119:11 in your life?

_____

_____

5. Match the following:

_____ Romans 8:2

_____ Romans 8:31

_____ Romans 8:6

_____ Romans 8:13

_____ Romans 8:7

a. "If you live according to the Spirit you put to death the deeds of the body."

b. "To be spiritually minded is life and peace."

c. "Jesus has made me free from the law of sin and death."

d. "The carnal mind is enmity against God."

e. "If God be for us, who can be against us?"

6. Read John 8:31,32.

a. What shall make you free? _____

_____

b. According to verse 31, what is the "truth?" _____

_____

7. What instruction did Jesus give the woman in John 8:11? _____

_____

8. What does John 8:12 mean to you? _____

_____

- You are a child of God. Ask God for the ability to walk holy before Him and others.

OVERCOMING TEMPTATION

Within the last 24 hours you have been tempted to sin and disobey God. This chapter will help you understand the purpose of temptation and reveal God's plan of escape to you. You can walk in victory and resist temptation every time. God calls you "more than a conqueror." Romans 8:37

1. The Bible clearly states that God doesn't tempt us. Where do the temptations you face come from? James 1:13-15.

a. (v. 14) _____

b. (v. 14) _____

2. The Bible lists three main types of temptations in 1 John 2:16. List them and a Bible character who gave into that particular temptation.

TEMPTATION	BIBLE CHARACTER
• the _____ of the _____	- _____
• the _____ of the _____	- _____
• the _____ of _____	- _____

3. Read 1 Corinthians 10:13 closely.

a. According to the above verse, are others experiencing the same temptations that you are facing? _____ yes _____ no

b. What will God be to you when you face temptations?

_____

c. List two things God will do for you while you are being tempted.

i. _____

ii. _____

d. In your own words, what does this verse say to you?

_____
_____
_____
_____

"Flee temptation and leave no forwarding address!"

4. Study 2 Samuel 11:1-4. What could King David have done to avoid committing adultery with Bathsheeba? In other words, how could he have "escaped?"

_____
_____
_____

5. Give a recent example of being tempted and yielding to the temptation. Then identify the "exit" door that God provided for you, but you failed to walk through it.

_____
_____
_____
_____

6. Read Genesis 39:7-12.

a. How did Joseph respond to this temptation? Genesis 39:7-12

_____
_____

b. What can you learn from his example?

_____
_____

"It is easier to stay out than to get out."
Mark Twain

7. Read Matthew 4:1-11. After Jesus' baptism He was led into the wilderness for a time of prayer. While there, the devil came and tempted Him. How did Jesus respond to the devil's temptations?

_____

_____

8. Given the above example of Jesus, why do you think it is important to meditate and memorize the Word of God?

_____

_____

_____

9. Read Psalm 119:11. What does this mean to you now?

_____

_____

_____

- Thank the Lord that according to the Bible there is no temptation that you cannot overcome.

- Ask Him to help you defeat the temptations you are facing right now. Remember, God is faithful!

PURITY OF HEART

God always looks at the heart. He desires for us to live pure lives before Him and others. There are incredible benefits to those who dare to live with a pure heart. This study will reveal those special blessings.

1. Find a dictionary and define "pure."

_____

_____

2. According to Matthew 5:8, what does God promise to those who have a pure heart?

_____

_____

3. Why do you think it is important to live a pure life before those who do not know Jesus as their Savior?

_____

_____

_____

> *"A holy life will produce the deepest impression.*
> *Lighthouses blow no horns, they only shine."*
> Dwight L. Moody

4. What does Psalm 24:3-5 say will be the benefit for those who live pure before God?

_____

_____

_____

> *A holy man is not one who cannot sin.*
> *A holy man is one who will not sin."*
> A.W. Tozer

5. Match the following from 1 Corinthians 6:15-20:

_____ temple of the Holy Spirit   a. Verse 17

_____ flee sexual immorality   b. Verse 19

_____ Holy Spirit who is in you   c. Verse 16

_____ glorify God with your body   d. Verse 18

_____ shall become one flesh   e. Verse 20

6. Read 2 Corinthians 6:11-18. What does Paul desire the Corinthian Christians not to do?

_____

_____

7. Read 2 Corinthians 7:1.

a. What are we to cleanse ourselves from? _____

_____

b. What are we to perfect? _____

_____

8. As we can tell, God is serious about purity. In Ephesians 5:3-5, list what is not appropriate for the child of God?

_____

_____

_____

9. In Ephesians 5:27, what kind of church does God want?

_____

_____

10. In 2 Timothy 2:22, what are we to "flee" and what are we to "pursue?"

_____

PURITY OF HEART
(PART 2)

You are well on your way to living holy before the Lord. Continue to dedicate your life afresh to Him everyday. There is a struggle over your allegiance. Resist the devil and he will run from you. Get closer to God and He will get closer to you! James 4:7-8

1. According to these passages of Scripture, what can you do to please the Lord?

1 Peter 1:22 _____

1 Peter 2:11 _____

2. Read Romans 13:14. Write how you can apply this scripture to your life?

_____

_____

_____

3. What should be our relationship with those who are not concerned with pleasing and obeying God? Proverbs 4:14,15

_____

_____

_____

4. Ephesians 4:22,23 gives you some helpful advice. What is it?

_____

_____

_____

5. Read Ephesians 5:8.

a. What was your life like before you met Jesus? _____

_____

b. What is your life like now? _____

_____

c. How should you walk now?

_____

_____

6. Look closely at 1 John 2:15,16.

a. What are we not to love? _____

_____

b. List the three things that are in the world.

i.   _____

ii.   _____

iii.   _____

c. In your own words list several things that might be considered
    "of the world."

_____

_____

_____

_____

7. The temptations you face are very difficult to overcome.
    However, what can you do according to Philippians 4:13?

_____

_____

8. Read Psalm 51:10. Stop and ask God to do the same in you!
    Now write how you feel.

_____

_____

_____

WEEK FOUR
(Days 22-28)

You are over half way on your *40 day* journey with the Lord. Don't give up! Stay faithful in your daily time with the Lord. Let Him speak to you. Remember, the devil wants you to quit. If you don't quit, you will win!

☐ Memory Verse – Mark 8:34

> ***"Whoever desires to come after Me, let him deny himself, and take up his cross, and follow me."*** **(NKJV)**

☐ Church Attendance

Church attended _____

How many times this week did you attend church _____

☐ Have you been baptized? If so, when and where _____
_____

☐ Met with Prayer Partner

☐ Did you have opportunity to share Jesus with anybody

Name(s) _____

☐ Prayer Requests
_____
_____
_____

☐ Answered Prayers
_____
_____
_____

WHAT DOES GOD WANT?

God wants a vibrant personal relationship with you. His aim is to help you become more like Jesus everyday. He desires to be your Lord and Master. In fact, God wants every area of your heart.

1. Romans 8:29 reveals a portion of God's plan for your life. What is it?

_____

_____

2. Explain what that means to you?

_____

_____

_____

3. According to Romans 6:13, what does God *not* want you to do and what does He *desire* for you to do?

_____

_____

_____

4. Pride is one of the reasons you do not surrender your life to the Lord. Why do you think God has a problem with pride?

_____

_____

_____

_____

5. Read Psalm 51:16,17.

a. What sacrifices will God not reject? _____

_____

b. What does it mean to have a broken and contrite spirit?_____

_____

c. How does one become broken and contrite?

_____

_____

_____

_____

6. Examine Isaiah 57:15 and list what God says He will do to and for the one who is broken and contrite.

a. _____

b. _____

c. _____

7. What does Paul say in Romans 12:1,2 that you should and should not do? List them.

a. (v. 1) _____

b. (v. 2) _____

c. (v. 2) _____

8. According to Matthew 22:37, what does Jesus want you to do?

_____

_____

_____

BEARING FRUIT

God calls His children to live a fruitful and productive life. In this study the heart of God will be revealed to you. You will see the importance God places on your ability to bear fruit for His glory. Don't forget that the closer you are to Him, the more He can do in and through you.

1. Spend some time reading and meditating on John 15:1-8.

a. (v. 1) Jesus is the _____. God is the _____.

b. (v. 2) What will God do to the branch that does not bear fruit?
_____

c. (v. 2) What will God do to the branch that bears fruit? Why?
_____
_____
_____

d. (v. 5) What must you do in order to bear fruit for Jesus?
_____
_____

e. (v. 7) What must you do in order to have prayers answered?
_____
_____

f. (v. 8) How is God glorified?
_____
_____

2. According to Psalm 1:1-3, what will cause you to bear fruit on a consistent basis?
_____
_____
_____

3. Write a statement explaining the truth of John 15:16.

_____

_____

_____

_____

4. According to Romans 7:4, for whom should we bear fruit?

_____

_____

5. What was Jesus' warning in Matthew 3:10?

_____

_____

_____

6. List the nine fruits of the Spirit in Galatians 5:22,23.

_____

_____

_____

_____

7. How are you able to determine if someone is a true Christian or not? Matthew 7:16,20

_____

_____

8. Match the following:

_____ fruit worthy of repentance   a. Romans 6:22

_____ good tree – no evil fruit   b. Luke 3:8

_____ you are known by your fruit   c. Matthew 7:18

_____ fruit unto holiness   d. Ephesians 5:9

_____ fruit of the Spirit   e. Luke 6:44

9. Paul told his friends to be what? Philippians 1:11

_____

_____

- Ask God each morning when you wake up to enable you to bear fruit for Him.

- Yield your body to His service and see what fruit comes forth.

ALWAYS FAITHFUL

There is nothing more honorable than faithfulness. In short, being faithful means you are committed to the end. In your new walk with God, He desires for you to remain loyal and faithful to Him. In doing so, you open yourself to the bountiful blessings of God. Frequently we are put into compromising situations. However, stay true to Him who died for you.

1. According to Psalm 31:23, what will God do to the faithful?

_____

_____

2. What will God do if you are faithful to Him all the days of your life? Revelation 2:10

_____

_____

3. What is God looking for on the earth?

2 Chronicles 16:9

_____

Psalm 101:6

_____

4. What does Jesus say about unfaithfulness in Luke 9:62?

_____

_____

"As you are faithful this one thing is certain the Lord will show you great and mighty things that you know not now."
Stanley Frodsham

5. What is the benefit of faithfulness? Proverbs 28:20

_____

6. What does God expect from His children? 1 Corinthians 4:2

_____

_____

7. What is required from those who wish to follow Jesus? Matthew 16:24

_____

_____

8. Describe the difference. Proverbs 13:17

   Wicked Messenger   _Faithful Ambassador_

_____   _____

9. Describe God's servant Caleb. What did God like so much about Caleb? Numbers 14:24

_____

_____

_____

10. Read Matthew 25:14-30 carefully.

a. (vv. 21, 23) How did Jesus reward faithfulness?

_____

_____

b. (vv. 28-30) How did Jesus say unfaithfulness will be rewarded?

_____

_____

_____

- Ask God for the power and fortitude to remain faithful to Him.

- Pray for the strength to resist all temptations that would cause you to compromise your commitment to Jesus.

- Remember God loves when His children are faithful to Him! FOREVER FAITHFUL!

BUILDING YOUR FAITH

1. According to Hebrews 11:1, what is faith?

_____

_____

_____

2. How does faith develop? Romans 10:17

_____

_____

3. Considering the above, what are some steps you can take to develop and grow your faith?

a. _____

b. Going to church and listening to the Word of God taught and preached.

c. _____

d. _____

4. Put Mark 9:23 in your own words.

_____

_____

_____

> *"It is when active faith dares to believe God*
> *to the point of action, that something has to happen."*
> Kathryn Kuhlman

5. Read Mark 11:24. What does Jesus say will happen to those who pray and believe?

_____

_____

_____

6. According to 2 Corinthians 5:7, how should the Christian now walk?

_____

7. Read Romans 4:20-21. Abraham received a promise from God. What do these verses teach us about faith and the faithfulness of God?

_____

_____

_____

8. Examine James 5:15.

a. Describe what you believe to be the prayer of faith. _____

_____

_____

b. What will be the result when you pray the prayer of faith?

_____

_____

9. What will keep you and others from seeing the power of God from working in your life?

_____

10. Read Luke 18:35-43.

a. What was the man's condition? (v. 35) _____

_____

b. What did he want Jesus to do for him? (v. 41) _____

_____

c. What did Jesus say caused the man to be healed? (v. 42) _____

_____

"Faith begins where the will of God is known."
F.F. Bosworth

BUILDING YOUR FAITH
(PART 2)

It is not your need that causes God to stop and take notice of your situation. Everybody has needs. As you will find in the examples below, it wasn't the need that caused God to stop. It was the faith. If you want to get God's attention, exercise your faith.

1. In Mark 5:25-34 a woman is healed of a twelve-year blood disease. According to Jesus, why was she healed?

(v. 34) _____

2. Where should our faith reside? Mark 11:22

_____

3. According to Mark 11:23, what will happen if we have faith?

_____

_____

"You get faith by studying the Word.
Study that Word until something in you 'knows that you
know' and that you do not just hope that you know."
Carrie Judd Montgomery

4. Please match the following:

_____ Hebrews 11:30   a. "Without faith it is
                              impossible to please God"

_____ Hebrews 11:39   b. "By faith we understand
                              the world was framed by
_____ Hebrews 11:3   the Word of God"

                         c. "By faith the walls of
_____ Hebrews 11:6   Jericho fell"

                         d. "They obtained a good
                              testimony through faith"

5. What does your faith help you to do?

_____

_____

6. In Hebrews 4:2 a reason is given for the Israelites not being saved. Give the reason.

_____

_____

DON'T MISS THIS:
There are things the Lord has planned for every Christian. God is a good God and wants to bless His children. However, the promises from the Word of God must be received by faith. If the Word of God is not mixed with your faith, then the promises of God cannot be received.

7. Read Ephesians 2:8,9. How does one enter into the family of God?

_____

_____

8. What did Jesus mean by what he spoke in Mark 9:23?

_____

_____

_____

9. List three things you are believing God to do in your life.

a. _____

b. _____

c. _____

"We tend to get what we expect."
Norman Vincent Peale

10. The writer in Hebrews 10:23 gives us the reason why we can continue to believe God, even when things don't seem to be going our way. What reason did he give?

_____

_____

_____

- This week look for opportunities to enlarge your faith.

- Let the Word of God invade your spirit. This will build your faith.

BECOMING A DISCIPLE

A disciple is an individual who has not only come into a relationship with God, but who is teachable and willing to receive instruction from God. It is possible for a person to be a believer, but never reach the level of a disciple. The difference is found in the intensity of hunger in a person. Does a person want a general relationship with the Lord or does he desire a deeper relationship, such as that between a father and a son?

In the New Testament a disciple was a "learner." The term applies to a person who has learned certain principles from another and maintains them on another's authority. In other words, a disciple goes beyond mere confession to a change in lifestyle, priorities and passions. Jesus is looking for modern day *disciples!*

1. What did Jesus say to Matthew that changed his life?
    See Matthew 9:9.

    _____

    _____

2. In Luke 14:26-27, Jesus lists a couple of issues that hinder people from becoming a disciple. What are those issues?

    a. (v. 26) _____

    b. (v. 27) _____

3. Describe what Jesus said should characterize His disciples:

    John 8:31 _____

    John 13:34-35 _____

    John 15:8 _____

4. Look at Luke 9:23-26.

a. Jesus gave three requirements to be His disciple. What are they?

    i. _____

    ii. _____

    iii. _____

b. What does verse 24 mean to you?

_____

_____

_____

5. In your opinion, what is the difference between a Christian and a disciple?

_____

_____

_____

6. Check the statements below that best describe a true disciple.

_____ Sets his heart to please others

_____ Sets his heart to please Jesus at all times

_____ Will suffer if need be to follow Christ

_____ Will obey the Bible when it is convenient

_____ Longs to tell others about Jesus

7. Read Proverbs 4:23. As a disciple it is important to keep our hearts pure. Why?

_____

_____

TAMING THE TONGUE

The tongue may be the enemy's greatest weapon. Many relationships, homes and careers have been destroyed because of the tongue. This chapter will help you understand how God wants to use your tongue to be a blessing and help to others.

1. Read James 3:3-12.

a. What do verses 3-6 tell you about your tongue?

_____

_____

_____

_____

b. Rewrite verse 8 in your own words.

_____

_____

_____

_____

c. According to verses 9-12, what should not be happening with your tongue?

_____

_____

_____

_____

2. According to Ephesians 4:29, what kind of things should come out of your mouth?

_____

_____

_____

_____

3. What does your speech reveal about your heart?
Matthew 12:34-35

_____

_____

_____

4. How can you put Colossians 4:6 into practice?

_____

_____

_____

_____

5. What does Proverbs 12:19 say about the tongue?

_____

_____

"Your life will move in the direction of your words."
Mike Murdock

6. How much power do your words have? Proverbs 18:21

_____

_____

_____

7. Match the following:

_____ Refrain his tongue from evil   a. Proverbs 15:4

_____ Tongue of the wise is health   b. 1 Peter 3:10

_____ Guards his mouth   c. Proverbs 13:3

_____ A deceitful tongue   d. Psalm 120:2

_____ Tree of knowledge   e. Proverbs 12:18

8. How can you apply the truth of Proverbs 15:1 to your everyday life?

_____

_____

_____

_____

- Ask God right now to help you guard the words of your mouth.

- Pray for the strength to only speak words of life and blessing to others.

WEEK FIVE
(Days 29-35)

Isn't the Lord good? His faithfulness is everlasting. This week you will learn some principles from God's Word that will change your entire life. Be sure to check the boxes below and stay current with your memory verses. Remember, share Jesus with a friend.

☐ Memory Verses

> *"And you shall know the truth, and the truth shall make you free.."* John 8:32 (NKJV)

> *"And my God shall supply all your need according to His riches in glory by Christ Jesus."* Philippians 4:19 (NKJV)

☐ Church Attendance

Church attended _____

How many times this week did you attend church? _____

☐ Have you joined a church? ____ yes ____ not yet

☐ Met with Prayer Partner

☐ Share Jesus with someone

Name(s) _____

☐ Prayer Requests

_____
_____

☐ Answered Prayers

_____
_____
_____

96

FORGIVING OTHERS

You are never more Christlike than when you choose to forgive the one who has harmed you. To forgive is God's best for your life. This chapter will reveal your need to forgive those who have wronged you.

1. What will genuine love do? 1 Peter 4:8

_____

_____

2. According to Jesus' words in Matthew 6:14-15, what will the Father do if you forgive someone who has wronged you?

_____

(v. 14) What will be the result if you refuse to forgive others? _____

_____

3. How many times are we to forgive someone?
    Matthew 18:21-22 _____

> *"Forgiveness is the fragrance that the flower*
> *leaves on the heel of the one who crushed it."*
> Mark Twain

4. Read Ephesians 4:32. What three commands are we given?

a. _____

b. _____

c. _____

5. Bitterness can overcome a person's heart if he/she fails to forgive. According to Hebrews 12:15, what two things will bitterness do to a person?

a. _____

b. _____

6. What are we instructed to do in Colossians 3:13 and why?

_____

_____

_____

7. Read Romans 12:18-21. What does God want us to do in the following verses?

Verse 18 _____

_____

Verse 19 _____

_____

8. What does God say He will do about your situation? (v. 19)

_____

_____

9. What are we instructed to do to our enemies?

_____

_____

_____

10. How should you overcome the evil that others do to you? (v. 21)

_____

_____

_____

-   Take the next few minutes to ask the Holy Spirit to reveal those people whom you have not yet forgiven.

-   Now ask God for the ability to release and forgive those individuals. YOU WILL BE SET FREE!

MARKED TO SERVE

Every move Jesus made upon the earth demonstrated His purpose to serve mankind. Before He went to the cross, Jesus gathered His closest friends for a time of fellowship. It was here that He took a basin of water and a towel and washed the disciples' feet. Jesus set the example for us. Now let's serve each other with all of our hearts.

1. Look at Matthew 20:26. What did Jesus reveal to His disciples about greatness?

_____

_____

_____

_____

2. Look now at Matthew 20:27. What did Jesus say about wanting to be first?

_____

_____

_____

_____

3. Read Matthew 20:28. What did Jesus reveal to us about His own life?

_____

_____

_____

_____

"Do all the good you can, by all the means you can,
in all the ways you can, in all the places you can,
at all the times you can, to all the people you can,
as long as you ever can."
John Wesley

4. How can you apply the teaching of Jesus to your life right now?

_____

_____

_____

_____

5. What instruction do you receive from Galatians 5:13?

_____

_____

_____

6. How are we to love each other? Galatians 5:14

_____

_____

> **"Life is a lot like tennis – he who serves best seldom loses."**

7. Read Galatians 6:9,10.

a. What does God promise if we endure and do good to others?

_____

_____

b. Write in your own words how you can put verse 10 into practice.

_____

_____

_____

_____

> **"God can do tremendous things through people who don't care who gets the credit."**

8. In Mark 10:45 Jesus reveals His purpose for coming to earth. State that purpose.

_____

_____

9. Below is your serving list. Write down the names of three people whom God would have you serve. Your goal is to be a blessing to them. In the space provided, write how you can best serve and bless them.

Name #1 _____

My Action for Blessing

_____

_____

Name #2 _____

My Action for Blessing

_____

_____

Name #3 _____

My Action for Blessing

_____

_____

- Thank God right now for the opportunity to serve others.

- Jesus set the example for us.

- Ask Him for the strength and understanding of how to bless others.

LOVING GOD'S WAY

One of the most difficult things to do as a Christian is to walk in love with those around you. It is difficult, but possible. God gives us the strength through the Holy Spirit to enable us to walk as Jesus walked, forgive as He forgave and love as He loved.

1. What did God do that demonstrated His love for you?

Romans 5:8 _____

1 John 4:9,10 _____

John 3:16 _____

2. Read 1 Corinthians 13:4-8. List the characteristics of loving God's way.

_____
_____
_____
_____

3. Who does Jesus say that you should love? Luke 6:27

_____
_____
_____

4. Why do you think "loving your enemies" is important?

_____
_____
_____

5. Read Matthew 22:34-40.

a. What does verse 37 mean? _____

_____
_____

b. How can you apply verse 39 to your life? _____

_____

_____

*"If you have love in your heart, you always
have something to give."*

6. Jesus spoke clearly about the importance of loving one another. What was He saying to His disciple in John 13:34,35?

_____

_____

_____

_____

7. Sometimes we say we love one another, but fail to show it with our deeds. What does 1 John 3:16-18 say about that kind of attitude and behavior?

_____

_____

_____

_____

-   It is difficult to love everyone at all times. Right now, ask God to help you love those you have a difficult time loving.

-   He will enable you to love the unlovable.

-   God will give you the strength to demonstrate His love to them.

GOD AND YOUR MONEY
(PART 1)

God has a lot to say about money. There are 500 verses on prayer, 500 verses on faith and over 2000 verses that address the issue of money. Did you know twenty percent of the Bible addresses money and money management? In fact, 16 out of Jesus' 38 parables deal with money. In this study you will discover God's view of money and His direction for your own finances. Prepare yourself. You are going to be blessed and challenged!

1. What does Haggai 2:8,9 say about God's attitude regarding money?

   _____

   _____

2. Psalm 35:27 reveals the heart of God about money and you. What is it?

   _____

   _____

   _____

3. Read Deuteronomy 8:18.

a. What does God empower us to do? _____

   _____

b. Why? _____

   _____

4. According to our study thus far, is God against you becoming blessed financially? _____ yes _____ no

5. According to Deuteronomy 28:1,2, what will cause you to supernaturally abound in the blessings of the Lord?

   _____

   _____

_____

_____

6. Put Proverbs 10:22 in your own words.

_____

_____

_____

7. What is God's warning to you in Psalm 62:10?

_____

_____

8. Read 1 Timothy 6:9-10.

a. (v. 9) What does Timothy say will happen to those who use all of their time and energy to become rich?

_____

_____

b. (v. 10) What is the "root of all evil?" _____

9. How will acquiring wisdom benefit you in attaining wealth? Proverbs 8:12-18

_____

_____

_____

_____

GOD AND YOUR MONEY
(PART 2)

The devil doesn't want you to prosper. John Avanzini says it best, "Satan is not nearly as concerned with driving you backwards as he is with CONTAINING you where you are, and KEEPING you from getting where God wants you to go." This chapter will help you have the mind of God when it comes to your finances. With God's help you can bust through the "spirit of containment."

1. What does God say will happen to you when you practice Psalm 1:1-3?

_____

_____

_____

2. Why do you think borrowing money is not a good thing? Proverbs 22:7

_____

_____

3. Give an example of when you borrowed money and later realized you had made a mistake.

_____

_____

_____

4. What will cause you to have plenty? Proverbs 21:5

_____

_____

5. Read Proverbs 21:20. Describe the difference between a wise person and a foolish person.

Wise   _Foolish_

_____   _____

_____   _____

6. Put Luke 12:15 into your own words.

_____

_____

_____

7. Read Matthew 6:33.

a. What should be our highest priority? _____

_____

_____

b. What will be the result? _____

_____

_____

8. List one of the reasons we get up and go to work each day?
    Ephesians 4:28

_____

_____

_____

9. How can you put Ephesians 4:28 into practice today?

_____

_____

_____

_____

-   It is a beautiful thing to have the mind of God when it comes to your money.

-   Thank God right now for your prosperity and blessings.

-   You are on the road to good success.

GOD AND YOUR MONEY
(PART 3)

According to theologians, the tithe was established 400 years before the law was given to Moses. It is God's will that all of His children bring a tithe to their place of worship. Some may ask, "what is a tithe?" A tithe is 10% of your income. This is God's way of seeing if your heart and life completely belong to Him. It is true that finances are one of the hardest things to surrender to God. When God is in charge of your finances, then the chances are He has ALL of you. In the questions to follow, you will realize the importance of obeying God in this area of your life. The rewards are outstanding. Be ready to see God work in your life and finances like never before.

1. Read Proverbs 3:9-10.

a. In your own words, what does verse 9 mean to you? _____
_____

b. What will be the benefit? (v. 10) _____
_____
_____

2. Take a close look at Proverbs 11:24-25. What truths come alive in each of these two verses?

Verse 24 _____
_____
_____
_____

Verse 25 _____
_____
_____
_____

3. What is meant by *"he who waters will be watered himself?"* Proverbs 11:25

_____

_____

_____

_____

4. Read Malachi 3:8-11.

a. (v. 8) If one fails to tithe his/her income, what does God say they are doing to Him? _____

b. (v. 9) What does God say will be the result of not tithing? _____

_____

In your opinion, what does this mean to you?

_____

_____

_____

_____

c. (v. 10) What are we commanded to do and why? _____

_____

_____

d. (v. 10) What will God do for us if we give 10% of our income to Him? _____

_____

_____

_____

_____

e. (v. 10) Does God want you to "try" or "test" Him in this area of your life?

_____ yes   _____ no

5. What does God say will happen to the person that gives generously? Luke 6:38

_____
_____
_____

6. What does God promise us if we are faithful in our giving?
   Philippians 4:19

_____
_____

7. Read 2 Corinthians 9:6-8.

a. (v. 6) What happens if you give little? _____
_____

b. (v. 6) What happens if you give much? _____
_____

c. (v. 7) What kind of giver does God love? _____

d. (v. 8) What is God able to do for you after you give unto Him?

_____
_____
_____
_____
_____

- This Sunday and every Sunday you have the opportunity to bring your tithe to the Lord. Trust God. Be strong and have faith.

- God will not fail you. In fact, you will be amazed at how God comes through for you. He will truly open the windows of heaven over your life.

HEAVEN: OUR ETERNAL HOME (PART 1)

The Word of God has a lot to say about heaven. One day each of us will take our last breath here on this earth. Our last breath here will be our first breath in heaven. Let this study warm your spirit as you look forward to your eternal home with Jesus.

1. Read John 14:1-3.

a. (v. 1) The disciples were obviously concerned about Jesus' announcement of His departure. What did He tell them?

_____

_____

b. According to verse 2, where was Jesus going and what would He be doing there? _____

_____

c. What was Jesus' promise to His disciples in verse 3? _____

_____

2. What two things will happen to the person who dies knowing Jesus as their Savior?

a. _____

b. _____

"A funeral among men is a wedding feast among the angels."
Kahlil Gibran

3. What does this verse reveal about heaven? 1 Corinthians 2:9

_____

_____

_____

4. According to Proverbs 14:32, what blessing do the righteous have when they die?

_____

_____

5. Why did Paul write that he could endure this earth's sufferings and hardships? Romans 8:18

_____

_____

_____

6. Why do you think Psalm 116:15 is true?

_____

_____

_____

7. Read 2 Timothy 4:6-8.

a. (v. 7) Paul mentioned three specific things he did while on this earth. List them.

_____

_____

_____

b. (v. 8) What is laid up for Paul and every believer that serves God faithfully?

_____

_____

> *"This world is the land of the dying;*
> *the next is the land of the living."*
> Tryon Edwards

8. What will God do when you get to heaven? Revelation 21:4

_____

_____

9. According to the above verse, what will not be allowed into heaven?

_____

_____

_____

- Isn't it wonderful that Jesus was and is victorious over death?

- Praise Him because of His wonderful power!

- Because He lives, we to shall live!

WEEK SIX
(Days 36-40)

Just five days remaining. Congratulations! You did it. The goal of this book is to help you follow Christ daily. No doubt there have been a lot of changes in your life over the recent days. This is just the beginning. God wants to make you more like Jesus everyday. Let him have His way in your life!

☐ Memory Verse – Matthew 6:33

"But seek first the kingdom of God and His righteousness, and all these things shall be added to you."
(NKJV)

☐ Church Attendance

Church attended _____

How many times this week did you attend church? _____

☐ Have you joined a church? ____ yes ____ not yet

☐ Met with Prayer Partner

☐ Share Jesus with someone

Name(s) _____

☐ Prayer Requests

_____
_____

☐ Answered Prayers

_____
_____
_____

HEAVEN: OUR ETERNAL HOME (PART 2)

Think about it. Right now Jesus is preparing a place for you in heaven (John 14:1-3). Can you imagine how beautiful it is going to be?

1. According to 1 John 3:2, what will we be like in heaven?

_____

_____

2. Read Isaiah 25:8.

a. What will God do to death? _____

b. What will God do to us? _____

3. What will take place after a person dies? Hebrews 9:27

_____

_____

4. In your own words, explain the truth of John 11:25,26.

_____

_____

_____

_____

5. Read John 3:36.

a. What will happen to the person who dies believing in Jesus?

_____

b. What will happen to the person who dies without Jesus?

_____

"There is no death. Only a change of worlds."

117

6. In Revelation 2:10 there is a command and a promise. List them.

a. Command _____

_____

b. Promise _____

_____

7. What did John see in Revelation 21:1,2?

_____

_____

_____

8. What do you think will be the greatest things about heaven? List at least three.

_____

_____

_____

_____

_____

9. Do you know anyone who is in heaven? If so, what do you think that person is doing?

_____

_____

_____

_____

10. Read Hebrews 12:1-2.

a. Who do you think is looking at us from that cloud of witnesses?

_____

_____

b. Because we have a heavenly audience, what should we do with the rest of our lives on earth?

_____

_____

_____

_____

_____

- Go ahead and thank God that you are on your way to heaven.

- Rededicate your life to Jesus so you can please Him.

- You may only have a few days left on this earth, so live it for Him! Finish your race with passion!

ENDURING TO THE END

Right now you may feel that the devil is hard after you. In fact, he is. He wants you to go back to the old lifestyle you once lived. A part of you may want to give up. Even quit. However, you know that you have come too far to quit now. Jesus has done so much in you - don't walk away from Him. If you will endure the race, it will be worth the sacrifice. Listen, you are being tested. That's right. You are going through a time of testing, but you can pass the test. Press on!

1. What does Paul's statement in Galatians 6:9 tell us we should do during times of testing?

    _____

    _____

2. What is God's promise to you if you endure?

    _____

3. According to Romans 5:3-4, what do hard times produce?

    _____

    _____

"By perseverance the snail reached the ark."
Charles H. Spurgeon

4. What instruction does the believer receive from 1 Corinthians 15:58?

    _____

    _____

    _____

5. Read Hebrews 10:23.

a. What are we encouraged to do? _____

    _____

b. Why? _____

6. James 1:2-4 gives us reasons why we must not quit when
    things get tough. List those reasons below.

_____
_____
_____
_____

> *"The human spirit is never finished when it is*
> *defeated...it is finished when it surrenders."*
> Ben Stein

7. What must we do? 2 Timothy 2:3

_____

8. How can 2 Corinthians 4:17,18 help you when you are going
    through difficult times?

_____
_____
_____

9. What are we instructed to do when we want to quit?
1 Timothy 6:12

_____
_____
_____

10. Read Proverbs 24:10. What does this mean to you?

_____
_____
_____

> *"The nose of the bulldog is slanted backwards so*
> *he can continue to breathe without letting go."*
> Winston Churchill

- If you will endure and continue with Jesus, you will overcome.

- Ask God now for the ability to persevere.

- Remember, you never win by quitting. There is too much at stake.

- Stay the course and fight the good fight of faith!

SPIRITUAL GIFTS

In church, you may have heard the phrase "spiritual gifts."
Perhaps you do not know what the church people are talking
about. This chapter will help you understand how God has gifted
you and the church to carry out His purposes upon the earth.

1. What does Ephesians 4:7-8 say Jesus did when He ascended?

_____

_____

_____

2. Read Ephesians 4:11-16.

a. (v. 11) List five of the gifts He gave.

_____

_____

_____

_____

c. (vv. 12-16) List at least four reasons why God gave the above
gifts to the body of Christ.

_____

_____

_____

_____

3. Read 1 Corinthians 12:1-11.

a. (vv. 8-10) List the gifts that are discussed.

_____

_____

_____

_____

b. (v. 11) Who distributes the gifts?

_____

4. According to Romans 12:6, will everyone have the same spiritual gift? _____ yes _____ no

5. List the gifts that are mentioned in Romans 12:6-8.

_____

_____

_____

_____

_____

6. How should we use the gifts that we have received from God? 1 Peter 4:10

_____

_____

7. What are we to desire? 1 Corinthians 12:31

_____

8. In your opinion, what do you believe to be the most desirable gifts?

_____

_____

_____

9. What gift(s) have you seen active or operating in your life?

_____

_____

_____

_____

- Pray now and thank God for the gift(s) He has given you.

- Ask Him for the wisdom on when and how to use those gifts.

- God will give you the exact gift when you need it to bring glory and honor to His name. However, you must have faith in God.

THE KEY TO SUCCESSFUL LIVING: WISDOM

If there is one thing you need above all else, it is wisdom. God is more than ready to disperse this great treasure upon you. It is for the asking. This study will reveal the wonderful benefits and blessings of a wisdom-filled life.

1. What two things are we told to get in Proverbs 4:5?

_____

_____

2. Match the following:

_____ Cannot be compared   a. 1 Corinthians 3:19

_____ Wisdom rests   b. Ephesians 1:17

_____ Fear of the Lord   c. Psalm 111:10

_____ Spirit of wisdom   d. Proverbs 14:33

_____ Wisdom of this world   e. Proverbs 8:11

3. What must you do first in order to become wise? Proverbs 9:10

_____

_____

According to Luke 2:52, when Jesus was a child He increased in what areas of His life? _____

_____

_____

4. What are we instructed to do in Colossians 4:5?

_____

_____

_____

127

"A single conversation across the table with a wise man is worth a month's study of books."
Old Proverb

5. Why do you think we need wisdom?

_____

_____

_____

6. Read James 1:5-8.

a. (v. 5) What must we do in order to receive wisdom from God?

_____

b. (v. 5) What does God desire to do for you?

_____

_____

c. In verse 6, what requirement must be met in order to receive wisdom from God?

_____

_____

d. (v. 8) What are we called if we fail to ask God in faith?

_____

_____

7. There is no doubt that wisdom is a necessity. What will be your state of being after you embrace and grow in wisdom? Proverbs 3:13

_____

_____

_____

"Knowledge leads us from the simple to the complex. Wisdom leads us from the complex to the simple."

8. What characteristics and benefits of wisdom are discussed in Proverbs 3:13-19. List five of them.

a. _____

b. _____

c. _____

d. _____

e. _____

- Now is a great time to ask God for heavenly wisdom.

- Believe and you will receive.

- Thank Him for this marvelous gift.

"CHANGING THE WORLD ONE LIFE AT A TIME"

There are over 6.4 billion people on the earth and 3.6 billion of those people have never heard a clear presentation of the gospel. Think about it, half the world's population has never had the opportunity to receive Jesus into their life. This breaks the heart of God. He desires everyone to know His son, Jesus. The question is: "What are you going to do about it?"

1. For whom did Jesus come and die? John 3:16

   _____

   _____

2. What motivated God to send His only Son to the earth?

   _____

   _____

3. Matthew 28:19-20 and Mark 16:15 are known as the "Great Commission." As Christians, what does God expect you to do?

   _____

   _____

   _____

   _____

> *"World vision is getting on your heart what is on God's heart – the world."*
> Dawson Trotman

4. Jesus saw the masses of humanity. What did He ask His disciples to pray? Matthew 9:36-38

   _____

   _____

   _____

   _____

5. What did Jesus mean in the following passages? John 17:18 and 20:21

John 17:18 _____

_____

John 20:21 _____

_____

How can you apply what Jesus said to your life? In other words, what are some of the ways you can "go into all the world?"

_____

_____

_____

_____

6. Read John 4:35. What does this reveal about the condition of the world?

_____

_____

_____

7. Usually, the last words someone speaks on earth reveal their heart and desire. What does Acts 1:8 reveal about Jesus' heart and desire for your life?

_____

_____

_____

_____

_____

8. According to 2 Thessalonians 1:8-9 and Revelation 20:12,15, why must we move quickly to tell the world about Jesus?

_____

_____

_____

_____

_____

9. Read 2 Peter 3:9. What does this say about the Father's heart?

_____

_____

_____

_____

10. In the next 18 months, what is your plan to go into all the world?

_____

_____

_____

_____

QUESTION:
How many people will be in heaven because of your influence?

Made in the USA
Lexington, KY
10 November 2019

56721457R00074